Published by Jaico Publishing House
A-2 Jash Chambers, 7-A Sir Phirozshah Mehta Road
Fort, Mumbai - 400 001
jaicopub@jaicobooks.com
www.jaicobooks.com

Published in arrangement with
The Creative Company
123 South Broad Street
Mankato, MN 56001
USA

Design and production by The Design Lab
Art direction by Rita Marshall

Photographs by Alamy (Mike Hill),
Corbis (Gallo Images, Gopal Chitrakar/Reuters,
Kevin Schafer), Getty Images (Rogerio Assis, Ira Block,
Tim Graham, Thorsten Milse, Michael K. Nichols/
National Geographic, Joel Sartore/
National Geographic, Art Wolfe),
iStockphoto (Eric Isselée)

MONKEYS
ISBN 978-81-8495-338-1

First Jaico Impression: 2012

Printed by
Aegean Offset Printers
220 B, Udyog Kendra – 1,
Greater Noida, UP - 201306, India

AMAZING ANIMALS

MONKEYS

VALERIE BODDEN

JAICO PUBLISHING HOUSE
Ahmedabad Bangalore Bhopal Bhubaneswar Chennai
Delhi Hyderabad Kolkata Lucknow Mumbai

Monkeys look different in different parts of the world

Monkeys are **mammals** with long arms and legs. Monkeys are smart. They are good climbers. There are many kinds of monkeys.

mammals animals that have hair and drink milk from their mother as babies

Monkeys have long tails. Some monkeys can hang from their tails. Monkeys have different fur colors. Some are brown or black. Others are white or gray. Monkeys have strong hands and feet. They can bend their fingers and toes to help them climb.

Some monkeys can use their tail like an extra hand

Monkeys come in many sizes. The smallest monkeys are only as long as a ruler. They weigh less than a can of soup. The biggest monkeys can weigh more than 100 pounds (45 kg)!

Most monkeys are small enough to easily climb trees

These Old World monkeys live in trees in Africa

Many monkeys live on the **continents** of Africa and Asia. They are called Old World monkeys. Other monkeys live in Central or South America. They are called New World monkeys. **Rainforests** are home to many kinds of monkeys. Other monkeys live in **swamps**. Monkeys usually live in trees.

continents Earth's seven big pieces of land

rainforests forests with many trees and lots of rain

swamps areas of land where the ground is wet and there are lots of trees

Monkeys eat plants and animals. Some monkeys like fruit and nuts. Others like to eat bugs or birds. Some monkeys like to eat flowers.

Monkeys spend most of their time climbing and eating

Mother monkeys show their babies how to get food

Most monkey mothers have one baby at a time. The babies are born with their eyes open. Sometimes other older monkeys help "babysit" young monkeys. Wild monkeys can live 15 years or longer.

Grooming helps keeps monkeys clean and healthy

Monkeys spend most of their day climbing in trees. Young monkeys play together. They pretend to fight. Grown monkeys **groom** each other's fur. Or they look for food.

groom get rid of dirt and bugs

Monkeys live in groups. Some of the groups are small. Other groups can have more than 100 monkeys in them. The groups can get very loud! The monkeys whistle and chirp. Some monkeys chatter or howl.

Monkeys in big groups go looking for food together

People around the world love monkeys. Some people even keep small monkeys as pets. Other people go to the zoo to see monkeys. These playful animals are lots of fun to watch!

This Old World monkey has a very big nose

A Monkey Story

Why do monkeys look like people? People on the continent of Africa used to tell a story about this. They said that one year a long time ago, there was not much food. The people put all of their food in a safe place. They had strong men guard it. Some of the men stole the food. So the people used magic to turn the men into animals that would look almost like people—monkeys!

Read More

Macken, JoAnn Early. *Monkeys*. Milwaukee: Weekly Reader Early Learning, 2002.

Steedman, Scott. *Amazing Monkeys*. New York: Knopf, 1991.

Web Sites

Enchanted Learning: Monkeys
http://www.enchantedlearning.com/themes/monkeys.shtml
This site has monkey activities, facts, and coloring pages.

Mindy's Memory Sanctuary
http://mindysmem.org/meet.html
This site has pictures and videos of monkeys.

Index